A Trip to the Zoo

THIS EDITION

Produced for DK by WonderLab Group LLC
Jennifer Emmett, Erica Green, Kate Hale, *Founders*

Editor Maya Myers; **Photography Editor** Kelley Miller; **Managing Editor** Rachel Houghton;
Designers Project Design Company; **Researcher** Michelle Harris; **Copy Editor** Lori Merritt;
Indexer Connie Binder; **Proofreader** Susan K. Hom; **Series Reading Specialist** Dr. Jennifer Albro

First American Edition, 2025
Published in the United States by DK Publishing, a division of Penguin Random House LLC
1745 Broadway, 20th Floor, New York, NY 10019

Copyright © 2025 Dorling Kindersley Limited
25 26 27 10 9 8 7 6 5 4 3 2 1
001–345892–July/2025

All rights reserved.
Without limiting the rights under the copyright reserved above, no part of this publication may be reproduced, stored in or introduced into a retrieval system, or transmitted, in any form, or by any means (electronic, mechanical, photocopying, recording, or otherwise), without the prior written permission of the copyright owner. Published in Great Britain by Dorling Kindersley Limited

A catalog record for this book is available from the Library of Congress.
HC ISBN: 978-0-5939-6643-3
PB ISBN: 978-0-5939-6642-6

DK books are available at special discounts when purchased in bulk for sales promotions, premiums, fund-raising, or educational use. For details, contact:
DK Publishing Special Markets, 1745 Broadway, 20th Floor, New York, NY 10019
SpecialSales@dk.com

Printed and bound in China
Super Readers Lexile® levels 310L to 490L
Lexile® is the registered trademark of MetaMetrics, Inc. Copyright © 2024 MetaMetrics, Inc. All rights reserved.

The publisher would like to thank the following for their kind permission to reproduce their images:
a=above; c=center; b=below; l=left; r=right; t=top; b/g=background

123RF.com: Elena Shchipkova / Lenor 24t, Smileus 16t; **Adobe Stock:** Jens 18t; **Alamy Stock Photo:** Richard Sowersby 28, 30bl, Michael Williams 27br; **Dreamstime.com:** Ali87cat 14, Bonita Cheshier 10-11, Famveldman 29, Frenta 30cla, Natalia Golovina 10, Hanohiki 25, Hupeng 1, Sergey Kokotchikov 8, Moodville 9, Nd3000 20, Nick Biemans / Nick.biemans 13, Mark Penny 22-23, Rien78 30tl, Sombra12 19, Popa Sorin 12, 30clb, Svetilo83 24b, Wirestock 21; **Fotolia:** Nazzu 11cr; **Getty Images:** AFP / Roslan Rahman 27c, FOAP / Cassie Skreblin 18b, Kyodo News 27bl, Stone / Paul Starosta 15, 30cl, VCG / Visual China Group 26; **Getty Images / iStock:** Amite 4-5, E+ / Kali9 3, Preflight 17; **Shutterstock.com:** Quiggyt4 6-7, Hayk_Shalunts 23c

Cover images: *Front:* **Dreamstime.com:** Miroslav Liska cl, Megan Lorenz b, Microvone clb, The Img (Background); **Getty Images / iStock:** Marta fernandez tr; *Back:* **Dreamstime.com:** Aleksandra Mikhailechko cra, clb

www.dk.com

This book was made with Forest Stewardship Council™ certified paper – one small step in DK's commitment to a sustainable future. Learn more at www.dk.com/uk/information/sustainability

A Trip to the Zoo

K.E. Lewis

Contents

6	Going on a Field Trip
10	Can You Say Safari?
14	Reptile House
18	In the Aviary
20	Under the Sea
24	Land of Ice
26	People at the Zoo
30	Glossary
31	Index
32	Quiz

Going on a Field Trip

Today, we're going on a field trip!

We are going to the zoo.

The zoo is home to many animals.

Some of those animals live on land. Some live in water.

People visit the zoo to see animals. They learn about animals, too.

Zoos protect endangered animals. These animals are at risk of becoming extinct.

Zoos care for animals rescued from the wild.

Asian elephants

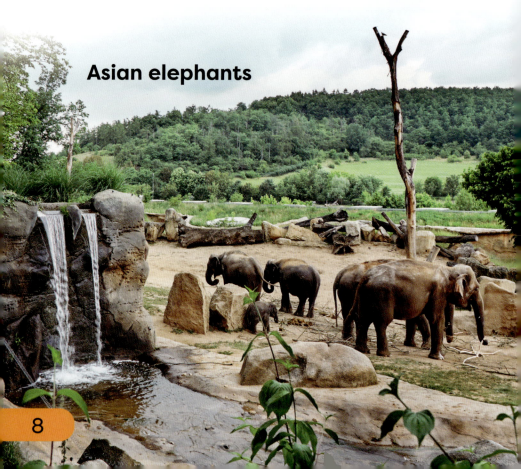

A natural habitat is where an animal lives in the wild. Natural habitats can have trees, mounds, water, and grass.

Zoos have habitats, too. People build boulders, caves, and waterfalls. They want to make the animals feel at home.

lions

Can You Say Safari?

Let's go on a zoo safari [suh-FAH-ree]! People go on safari to see animals from Africa.

See that ostrich running?

What about the giraffe eating from a tree?

Or that hippo in the water?

You might spy a zebra grazing. A lion sunning on a rock. A meerkat peeping from its hole.

Thump! Thump! Hear the gorilla beating its chest?

These animals are all mammals. Mammals are warm-blooded.

Mammals are born live from their mothers. They drink milk from their mothers. They usually have hair or fur.

Humans are mammals, too!

Reptile House
Oh, SNAP!

Welcome to the Reptile House. Say hello to the American alligator!

Reptiles are cold-blooded. Their bodies need the sun to get warm.

Reptiles breathe air. Most reptiles have scales. Reptiles hatch from eggs.

western green lizard hatching

Aldabra giant tortoise

Turtles are reptiles. Tortoises, too.

Some tortoises can live for more than 100 years.

crested gecko

All lizards are reptiles. So are snakes. Hiss! Snakes are found on every continent except Antarctica.

green pythons

In the Aviary

Squawk! Chirp! Let's fly into the aviary [AY-vee-air-ee]. This is where the birds live.

scarlet macaws

Birds are warm-blooded, like mammals. They hatch from eggs, like reptiles.

Crack! Crack!

Birds' bodies are covered in feathers. They have wings and beaks.

American flamingo

Many birds live inside the aviary. And flamingos live right outside the door!

Under the Sea

Let's take a deep dive into the aquarium [ah-KWAIR-ee-um]!

The aquarium holds plants and animals that live in water.

Most of those animals are fish.

In the wild, some fish live in the ocean. The ocean has salt water.

tambaqui

Others live in rivers and lakes. Rivers and lakes have fresh water.

Small fish swim in groups called schools. Larger fish, like sharks, usually swim alone.

whale shark

Many fish live near a coral reef. Other animals live in tide pools.

Land of Ice

Brrrrrr! Polar bears live on ice. A walrus and a seal splash in the cold water.

These animals grow thick layers of fat called blubber. Blubber helps keep them warm.

Baikal seal

king penguins

Penguins waddle and slide on the ice. Special feathers help them stay warm, too.

giant pandas

People at the Zoo

You'll find people at the zoo, too. Zookeepers feed the animals. They keep the animals' habitats clean. They make sure the animals stay healthy.

Zookeepers give presentations for visitors. They share facts about animals. They show people how they care for animals.

Zoologists take care of animals, too. They study the animals. They discover things that can help animals in the wild.

Zoologists take care of injured animals. The animals get better. Then, they may go back to their natural habitats.

You can see your favorite animals at the zoo. And people can care for animals there, too. Zoos help us understand what animals need to survive in the wild.

Come back soon!

Glossary

aviary
a place where birds are kept

habitat
where an animal lives

hatch
to be born from an egg

safari
an adventure to see animals in their natural habitat

zoologist
a person who studies animals

Index

alligator 14

aquarium 20

aviary 18, 19

birds 18, 19

eggs 15, 18

endangered animals 8

fish 20, 21, 22, 23

flamingos 19

giraffe 11

gorilla 12

habitats 9, 26, 28

hippo 11

lions 9, 12

lizards 15, 17

mammals 13, 18

meerkat 12

ostrich 10

penguins 25

polar bears 24

reptiles 14, 15, 16, 17, 18

safari 10

seal 24

sharks 22

snakes 17

tortoises 16

turtles 16

walrus 24

zebra 12

zookeepers 26, 27

zoologists 28

Quiz

Answer the questions to see what you have learned. Check your answers with an adult.

1. What kind of animals are warm-blooded and have fur?
2. Name one reptile.
3. What do you call a group of small fish swimming together?
4. True or False: Some Arctic animals have blubber to keep them warm.
5. What do you call a person who feeds and takes care of animals in a zoo?

1. Mammals 2. Lizard, alligator, turtle, snake 3. School
4. True 5. Zookeeper